# My Room

by Deborah Akers
illustrated by Debbie Rigby

Scott Foresman
is an imprint of

Glenview, Illinois • Boston, Massachusetts • Mesa, Arizona
Shoreview, Minnesota • Upper Saddle River, New Jersey

**Illustrations**
Debbie Rigby

ISBN 13: 978-0-328-39308-4
ISBN 10: 0-328-39308-8



1 2 3 4 5 6 7 8 9 10 V010 17 16 15 14 13 12 11 10 09 08

This was my room
when I was a baby.
It had many things
to play with.

But I will get bigger.
My room will change.
Nothing stays the same.

This was my room
when I was three.
It had so many things.
I would play all day.

But I will get bigger.

My room will change.

Nothing stays the same.

I have become older.

This is my room now.

It has games and books.

It has everything I need.

My little sister always plays
with my old toys.
She likes my old books.
I am glad that I kept them!